My Hindu Year

Cath Senker

PowerKiDS
press.

New York

Published in 2008 by The Rosen Publishing Group, Inc.
29 East 21st Street, New York, NY 10010

First Edition

Picture Acknowledgments:
Art Directors & Trip Photo Library 13 (R. Belbin), 16 (Eric Smith), 17
(Resource Foto), 21, 23, 24 (H. Rogers); Britstock 4 (Hideo Haga);
Chapel Studios 20 (B. Mistry); Circa Photo Library *Cover*, 6 (John Smith), 7
(William Holtby), 8, 15, 27 (John Smith); Impact Photos *Title page* (Robin Laurence), 10
(J. L. Dugast), 14 (M. de Vries); Nutshell Media 5 (Yiorgos Nikiteas); World Religions 9
(C. Stout), 11, 12, 18 (P. Kapoor), 19, 22 (Christine Osborne), 25 (C. Stout), 26 (Nick Dawson).

Cover photograph: Having fun with paint and colored water at the Holi festival.
Title page: Children with painted faces for Holi.

Library of Congress Cataloging-in-Publication Data

Senker, Cath.
  My Hindu year / Cath Senker. -- 1st ed.
      p. cm. -- (A year of religious festivals)
  Includes bibliographical references and index.
  ISBN-13: 978-1-4042-3731-5 (library binding)
  ISBN-10: 1-4042-3731-3 (library binding)
  1. Fasts and feasts--Hinduism--Juvenile literature. I. Title.
  BL1239.72S46 2007
  294.5'36--dc22
                                        2006027795

Acknowledgments: The author would like to thank Dhara, Lata, Bhupendra and
Darshan Patel for all their help in the preparation of this book.

Manufactured in China

Contents

A Hindu life

Hindus believe there is one God. He is everywhere. God is always loving, but he can also get angry.

Hindus have many beliefs about God, the world, and the people in it. They see God in many forms, as gods and goddesses. Many Hindu festivals are about these gods and goddesses.

Images of Hindu gods in a temple, from left to right: Ganesha, Lakshmi, Durga, and Saraswati.

This is Dhara. She has written a diary about the Hindu festivals.

Dhara's diary
Sunday, October 11

My name's Dhara Patel. I'm eight years old. I've got a brother named Darshan, who's twelve. We live with our mom, dad, and grandmother. My dad's from Gujarat in India, and my mom's from Uganda, and before that Gujarat. My family is Hindu. At home, we always eat vegetarian food. I like dancing, painting, and playing with my friends. My favorite festival is Navaratri.

Hindus have lots of holy books, such as the *Vedas*. They teach people how to worship God.

The Hindu symbol is called Aum.

Daily worship

Every day

Hindus worship every day at home. Worship is called puja. Hindus have a shrine in their homes where they do puja.

At the shrine, Hindus make offerings to a murti. A murti is a sacred statue of God, or a god or goddess.

This girl is making an offering to an image of Krishna.

Hindus in India gathering at
the mandir for worship.

Hindus also go to the
mandir (temple) to worship.
Outside India, people
mainly gather at the
mandir on the
weekend.

Dhara's diary
Saturday, October 18

Today, we went to the mandir.
We sat down and prayed to
God. Afterward, we sang
songs. We always go to the
mandir to celebrate the
festivals. The best thing about
going there is eating delicious
food! We also have a shrine at
home where we worship every
day. There are murtis of the
gods Ganesha and Krishna, and
the goddess Saraswati.

Divali

October/November

Divali is a joyful festival of lights. It celebrates the return of Rama and Sita, in the story from the *Ramayana*.

The story shows how good wins over evil. People light divas (oil lamps) to welcome Rama and Sita.

This family has lit diva lamps in front of their shrine for Divali.

Rangoli patterns are often made in swirls or the shape of flowers.

Dhara's diary

Sunday, October 26

Yesterday was Divali. We had lights everywhere. I wore my *chaniya choli*, a beautiful dress I only wear on special occasions. We said "Happy Divali" to everyone. I entered a rangoli competition, but I didn't win. I got a trophy for dancing though. We went to the mandir and prayed for a good year. We shared sweets. Later, at home, we made poppadoms. Delicious!

At Divali, people make rangoli patterns from colored rice powder. They hope the goddess Lakshmi will see the beautiful patterns and visit their homes. Hindus pray to Lakshmi to bring them good luck in the coming year.

Saraswati Puja

January/February

This festival celebrates the goddess Saraswati and the first day of spring. Saraswati is the goddess of learning. She is also the goddess of music, poetry, dance, and drama.

People wear bright yellow clothes at this festival. Yellow stands for the warmth of spring.

The beautiful goddess Saraswati is shown playing an instrument called a vina.

Children playing traditional Indian instruments. The girl is playing the harmonium. The boy is playing the tablas.

In Bengal, people carry giant images of Saraswati around the streets. At the end of the day, they say goodbye to the images by placing them in the river. Music is played for all to enjoy.

Mahashivaratri

February/March

The name of this festival means "the Great Night of Shiva." It celebrates Shiva, one of the most important forms of God.

Mahashivaratri is a solemn festival. Some Hindu families fast. At the mandir, people pour milk over a stone column called the Shiva Linga. This is to honor Shiva.

A boy in India washing a Shiva Linga with milk.

A woman dancing a popular Indian dance for Mahashivaratri.

Shiva is also known as the "Lord of the Dance." Hindus believe he dances a special dance on Mahashivaratri.

Dhara's diary
Thursday, February 19

Yesterday was Mahashivaratri, Shiva's birthday. When Shiva dances, sometimes he shows his anger and sometimes his happiness. It was a fast day, which means we only ate certain foods. We fasted to clean our bodies. I helped to make sago patties, which are small white pies. We ate them with sweet potatoes. They were yummy. We didn't eat sugar, rice, or green vegetables. We broke our fast in the evening.

Holi

February/March

Holi is a joyful festival at springtime. There are bonfires, processions, music, and dancing.

Hindus remember the story of Lord Krishna, a form of God. When he was young, Krishna loved to play tricks and have fun. Krishna, his friends, and his relatives used to throw colored water over each other.

People in West Bengal, India, enjoying a water fight with colored water at Holi.

This boy in Britain is having fun spraying his friends with colored powder around the Holi bonfire.

At Holi people celebrate the love between Krishna and all living things. Children go out into the streets and splash each other with brightly colored water.

Dhara's diary
Sunday, March 7

Yesterday it was Holi. We went to the mandir wearing white clothes and threw colored water all over each other. We got completely covered in it! My friends played tricks, too, like hiding from each other. We did this to remember how Krishna loved playing tricks when he was young. Then we ate long noodles, boiled with sugar and ghee.

Ramnavami

March/April

Ramnavami is a happy festival. It celebrates the birthday of Rama, a form of God. He came down to Earth to stop evil in the world.

Rama is the hero of the famous story, the *Ramayana*. His faithful servant was Hanuman, the monkey king. Hanuman helped to rescue Rama's wife, Sita.

The *Ramayana* story being acted out in Indonesia. It is a very long performance.

This couple in India are dressed up as Rama (left) and Sita (right). They are the main people in the *Ramayana* story.

Dhara's diary
Thursday, April 1

On Tuesday, it was Rama's birthday. We dressed in our best clothes and went to the mandir. We bathed the murti of Rama in water and milk. Then we sang songs. Some people went to the mandir every day for seven days, but we just went once. I like the stories from the *Ramayana*. My favorite person is Sita.

At Ramnavami, people read or act out parts of the *Ramayana*. At the mandir, a murti of baby Rama is placed in a cradle.

Ratha Yatra

June/July

Ratha Yatra is a grand festival in India and England. In some places, thousands of Hindus join in.

Ratha Yatra means "the journey of the chariot." In Puri, East India, people pull three huge chariots through their town. There is a murti on each chariot.

Here in Puri, East India, the chariots have stopped to let people see the murtis.

The Ratha Yatra chariot at a procession in Britain. When Ratha Yatra is celebrated in Britain, there is usually just one chariot.

The murtis on the chariots are Jagannath, his brother and his sister. Jagannath is another name for Krishna. People tell stories about him and sing songs.

Dhara's diary
Saturday, June 19

Today, it was Ratha Yatra. A small procession went around a few streets near our home. Everyone gathered in their best clothes and there was dancing. Then everyone went home to cook some tasty food. In India, the roads are closed for the day of Ratha Yatra, because the processions are so big. I'd love to go to Ratha Yatra in India one day.

Raksha Bandhan

July/August

At Raksha Bandhan, brothers and sisters show their love for each other. Every sister marks her brother's forehead with a special paste. Then she puts rice grains on the mark.

She ties a rakhi around her brother's wrist. A rakhi is a bracelet made from thread. It is to protect him from evil.

This girl is tying a rakhi around her brother's wrist.

This brother and sister are giving each other delicious Indian sweets at Raksha Bandhan.

Dhara's diary
Sunday, August 31

Yesterday, it was Raksha Bandhan. I made a rakhi for my brother Darshan and tied it around his wrist. I gave him a blessing and he gave me some money. I felt proud of my brother yesterday. I also sent rakhis to my cousins Kunj and Kevin in Canada. When they come to visit, they'll give me a present.

The sister puts a sweet called barfi in her brother's mouth. He gives her a present and promises to look after her.

Krishna Janmashtami

August/September

This happy festival celebrates Krishna's birth. For some Hindus, this is the most important festival.

Hindus believe that Krishna was born at midnight. In the evening, they meet at the mandir. They move lamps in circles in front of the murtis. This is the arti ceremony.

These children are helping to perform the arti ceremony.

Baby Krishna (left) and his brother Balaram stealing buttermilk. It is said that Krishna loved milky foods.

People sing religious songs about Krishna, called bhajans. There is dancing too. Many Hindus fast all day until midnight. At midnight, they share fruit and sweets, or a big meal.

Dhara's diary
Tuesday, September 7

Last night, it was Krishna's birthday. We went to the mandir and sang songs. There was a cradle holding a murti of baby Krishna. At midnight, bells were rung to celebrate Krishna's birth. We took turns rocking the cradle. By then we were really hungry. We ate a proper meal at the mandir, with puris, rice, and dhal. It was delicious!

Ganesha Chaturthi

August/September

Ganesha is a popular god. He has an elephant's head. Many Hindu families have a murti of him at home.

For this festival, in Western India, people make clay images of Ganesha. They place them in their home shrines. At morning and evening prayers, they pray to Ganesha.

An image of Ganesha, the god of wisdom, good luck, and riches.

An image of Ganesha is carried
down to the lake in Gujarat, India.

Saturday, September 18

Today, we celebrated Ganesha Chaturthi at the mandir. We prayed to Ganesha and then to the other gods. We sat down and a group of people sang songs. Then we sang them too. Afterward, we ate a shared meal. Some people stayed in the mandir to pray again. We always pray to Ganesha at home. I pray to him if I'm worried about something.

Everyone enjoys singing bhajans, especially children. At the end of the festival, huge crowds carry the images of Ganesha to the sea, river, or lake. They plunge them into the water.

Navaratri

September/October

Navaratri means "nine nights."
At this lively festival, Hindus worship
different mother goddesses.

The main goddess is Lord Shiva's wife.
She is often called Parvati or Durga.

At the end of the festival, these Hindus in Bangladesh place an image of Durga in the river to say goodbye.

People dancing the stick dance, called *dandya ras*, at Navaratri.

Everyone dances around a special shrine. It has pictures of the mother goddesses on it. There are two special dances—a circle dance and a stick dance.

Hindus of all ages dance and sing into the night. Some people join in every evening for nine days!

Dhara's diary
Saturday, October 23

Navaratri is really fun. Last night, we went to the hall to dance. We made a circle with the goddesses in the middle and danced around them. Then some people sang, and others clapped. Next we did arti, and after that we did the stick dance. I was exhausted! Before we went home, we ate a good meal.

Festival calendar

October/November
Divali

The festival of lights.

January
Lohri

A one-day festival to celebrate the end of the winter season, celebrated mainly in Punjab, Northern India. Bonfires are lit.

January
Pongal

A three-day festival in Southern India that starts on exactly the same day as Lohri. It celebrates the rice harvest. Rice boiled in milk is offered to the sun god, Surya.

January/February
Saraswati Puja

A spring festival to worship Saraswati, the goddess of learning.

February/March
Mahashivaratri

The main festival to worship Shiva.

February/March
Holi

A spring festival. People spray each other with colored water and make bonfires.

March/April
Ramnavami

This festival celebrates Rama's birthday.

June/July
Ratha Yatra

A festival to worship Krishna. Huge chariots with images of Krishna, his brother, and his sister are pulled through the streets.

July/August
Raksha Bandhan

A special festival for brothers and sisters.

August/September
Krishna Janmashtami

The celebration of Lord Krishna's birthday.

August/September
Ganesha Chaturthi

The main festival for the worship of Ganesha.

September/October
Navaratri and Durgapuja

Celebrations of the mother goddess.

September/October
Dassehra

People act out the story of Rama's victory over the demon Ravana.

Glossary

arti Lighting candles and moving them in a circle. It is done in front of images of gods to honor them.

barfi A sweet made from milk and sugar.

bhajans Songs to glorify God. Musicians usually play along with the singers.

blessings God's help and protection.

diva A lamp made from twisted cotton wool dipped in melted butter. It is lit during worship. Many divas are lit at Divali.

Ganesha The god with an elephant head. He is kind to all living things.

ghee Oil made from melted butter.

Hanuman The monkey god.

honor To show that you admire and respect a person, or God.

Krishna One of the most popular forms of God, who came to Earth about 5,000 years ago.

Lakshmi The goddess of wealth.

mandir A place of worship for Hindus, sometimes called a temple.

murti This word means "form." It is the image or sacred statue of God, or a god or goddess, used in worship.

offerings Things that are offered to the image of a god, to ask for blessings.

puja Worship, at home or at the mandir. People usually worship at a shrine with images of gods and goddesses.

rakhi A bracelet, usually made from cotton or silk.

Rama The hero of the Ramayana story. He came to Earth as a form of God.

Ramayana One of the important Hindu holy books. It is a poem with 24,000 verses.

rangoli A beautiful pattern made at the entrance of homes and mandirs. The rangoli pattern is to welcome gods and visitors.

Saraswati The goddess of learning.

Sita Rama's wife.

Vedas Very old holy books that tell Hindus how to worship God.

For Further Reading

Books to Read

Hindu Stories (Traditional Religious Tales) by Anita Ganeri (Picture Window Books, 2006)

Hinduism (World Religions) by Ranchor Prime (Walrus Books, 2005)

Holi (Rookie Read-About Holidays) by Uma Krishnaswami (Children's Press, 2003)

The Kid's Book of World Religions by Jennifer Glossop (Kids Can Press, 2003)

What You Will See Inside A Hindu Temple by Dr. Mahendra Jani (Skylight Paths Publishing, 2005)

World Religions (History Detectives) by Simon Adams (Southwater, 2004)

Places to Visit

Asian Art Museum
200 Larkin Street
San Francisco, CA 94102
Tel: 415.581.3500
www.asianart.org/

Los Angeles County Museum of Art
5905 Wilshire Boulevard
Los Angeles, CA 90036
Tel: 323-857-6000
www.lacma.org

Metropolitan Museum of Art
1000 Fifth Avenue at 82nd Street
New York, NY 10028-0198
Tel: 212-535-7710
www.metmuseum.org

Rubin Museum of Art
150 West 17th Street
New York, NY 1001
Tel: 212-620-5000
www.rmanyc.org

Due to the changing nature of Internet links, Powerkids Press has developed an online list of Web sites related to the subject of this book. This site is updated regularly. Please use this link to access the list:
www.powerkidslinks.com/ayrf/hindu

The author
Cath Senker is an experienced writer and editor of children's information books.

Index